REA's Quick & Easy Guide to

Writing Your A+ Research Paper

Staff of Research & Education Association

Research & Education Association
Visit our website at
www.rea.com

Research & Education Association
61 Ethel Road West
Piscataway, New Jersey 08854
E-mail: info@rea.com

REA's Quick & Easy Guide to
WRITING YOUR A+ RESEARCH PAPER

Published 2008

Printed in the United States of America

Library of Congress Control Number 2001087211

ISBN-13: 978-0-87891-786-0
ISBN-10: 0-87891-786-1

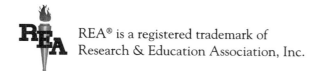
REA® is a registered trademark of
Research & Education Association, Inc.

sample title page

Title of Your Research Paper

Your Name

Name of Course

Instructor's Name

Date

TABLE OF CONTENTS

HOW TO USE THIS HANDBOOK

Its Uses:

This handbook has been written to be used (1) as an overview of the steps and skills needed to write a successful research paper, (2) as a specific guide to each step of the organizing, researching, composing, and editing processes, and (3) as a source for examples and rules of correct usage and writing structure.

To use the information presented in this handbook to best advantage, you should first read the entire book to become familiar with what goes into writing a research paper. Then, as you begin the process of writing your research paper, use this book to guide you through the specific steps as you complete them. During the composing, editing, and revising steps, you should reference the sections on grammar and correct sentence structure whenever you have a question about a sentence or word.

The Sections:

To enhance your understanding of the creation of a research paper, this handbook has been organized into three main sections: Developing the Subject, Gathering Material, and Writing the Paper. Each of these sections is placed in the chronological order you will encounter them as you write your research paper. As you complete each section, it would help you best to review the material in the section and double-check that you have completed all of the steps and understand all of the information presented. In doing this you not only use this book as a guide, but also as a checklist to make sure you have completed all of the steps necessary for creating a great research paper. A fourth section, Helpful Hints on Grammar and Writing, has been included as a reference for students encountering difficulties during the composing, editing, and revising stages of writing a research paper.

The Examples:

You should notice that examples of research paper pages are given throughout this handbook to visually aid you in preparing your paper. There are examples of a title page, outline, appendix, and bibliography. You should use these examples as models when creating your research paper. Your finished title page, outline, appendices, and bibliography should look very similar to examples provided in this handbook.

Throughout the text you will also notice examples of footnotes and bibliography formats. Once again, these examples have been provided to give you a visual reference of what the elements of your research paper will look like.

We have placed examples of reference indexes and menu screens from a computer library catalog. You should use these examples to familiarize yourself on the organization and wording of these sources before going to the library. If you know what to expect before you go to the library then you will be able to find what you are looking for faster, find more sources, and feel more confident that you have found all of the information available.

Finally, at the end of the handbook you will find a checklist. Use this checklist to double-check that every aspect of your research paper has been completed and included. Using this checklist should be the final step before submitting your research paper.

Sample Outline of a
Research Paper

I. Developing the Subject
    A. Choosing the Topic
        1. limiting the subject
        2. availability of materials
        3. interest in the subject
    B. The Relationship Between Topics, Purposes, and the Thesis
    C. Developing Organization for Your Topic
        1. chronological
        2. compare and contrast
        3. topical
        4. problem-solution
    D. Developing an Information Base for Your Topic
        1. general reading
        2. focused-free writing
        3. who, what, where, when, and why?
        4. list of ideas, questions, and responses
    E. Developing Your Thesis Statement
II. Gathering Material
    A. An Overview of the Steps and Sources
    B. General Reference Material
    C. Card and Computer Catalogs
    D. Indexes for Periodicals and Other Materials
    E. Bibliography Cards
        1. one-author books
        2. two-author books
        3. multiple-author books
        4. one-editor books
        5. one-translator books
        6. compilation books or anthologies
        7. periodicals
        8. encyclopedia articles
    F. Finding Usable Information
    G. Notecards
III. Writing the Paper
    A. Putting Your Notes into an Outline
    B. The Structure of a Research Paper
    C. Revising and Rewrites
        1. first draft
        2. second draft
        3. third draft
        4. additional drafts

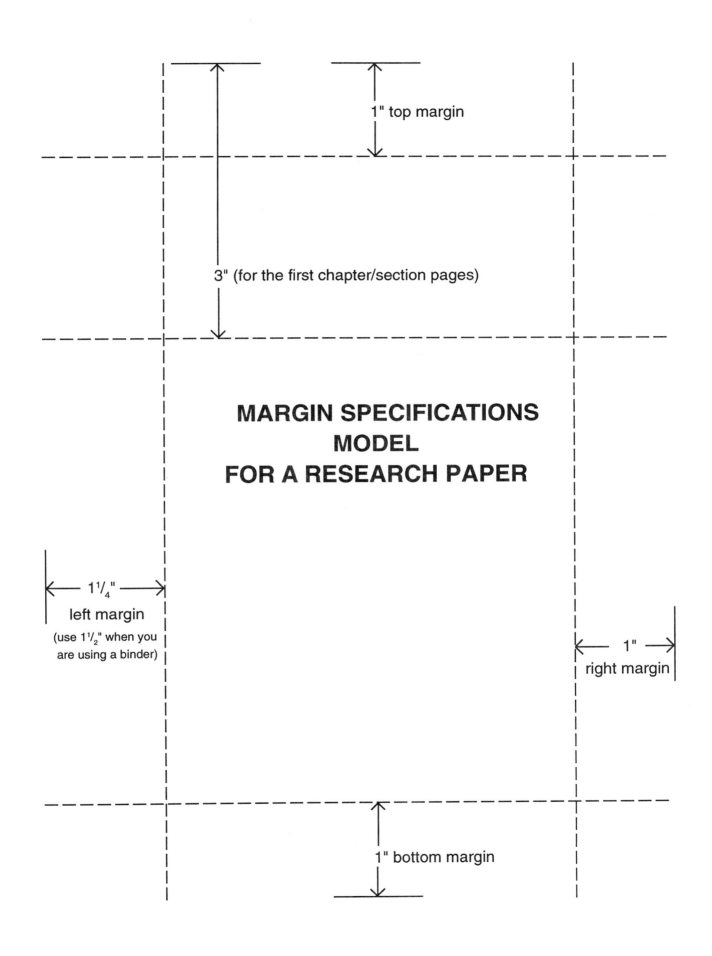

1" top margin

3" (for the first chapter/section pages)

**MARGIN SPECIFICATIONS
MODEL
FOR A RESEARCH PAPER**

$1\frac{1}{4}$" left margin

(use $1\frac{1}{2}$" when you are using a binder)

1" right margin

1" bottom margin

WRITING YOUR A+ RESEARCH PAPER

I. DEVELOPING THE SUBJECT

Choosing the Topic

Many things should influence the choice of your topic. When a professor assigns a research paper, certain restrictions are often placed on the student. If the length of the paper is established, this should have a direct bearing on the topic. For example, can the topic "Causes of World War II" be adequately treated in a three-page paper? A writer must learn to limit his or her topic. Also, does the topic lend itself to the assignment? Would such a theme as the influence of the Beatles on the sixties generation be an appropriate topic for a research paper? You must be able to answer these questions before any writing is done. But perhaps the most important question in the choice of a topic is interest. If a writer knows little about a topic, he or she must ask one basic question: "Do I have enough curiosity to investigate this topic further?" Nothing is more tedious than writing about something which is of no interest. This boredom is often expressed in the style of the writing and the reader will also suffer.

When deciding on an interesting topic on which to write, you must take into account another factor: availability of materials. A topic can be the most interesting subject in the world, but if you only have one 20-page book to use as a source for a 5,000-word research paper, that topic cannot be used. You must have access to useful books, reference books, and periodicals from which to collect information for the research paper. When you are about to make a decision on a topic, the amount of material available—meaning in nearby libraries—is a very important factor. Some preliminary library research and a knowledge of the topic can help in deciding whether there is sufficient material available to use a particular topic.

Many professors will assign topics to write about; others will allow students to choose their own topics. A topic is any subject of study, inquiry, or discussion that is addressed for the sake of an audience. A topic, however, is not a main point or a thesis. Remember that a topic is the subject about which the author writes. Books, cars, people, sports, rainbows, fish, potato chips—anything can be a topic of inquiry, study, or discussion. The point is to choose one and begin to focus on writing about it.

Some topics are too broad to deal with in a short 500-word paper so the professor may ask that the topic be narrowed. Narrowing a topic means limiting it and becoming more specific about what is to be discussed in the paper, making it a manageable length and scope.

The Relationship Between Topics, Purposes, and the Thesis

Research papers would be pointless without an audience. Why write a research paper if no one wants or needs to read it? Why add evidence, organize your ideas, or correct bad grammar? The reason to do any of these things is because someone out there needs to understand what you mean or say.

What does the audience need to know in order to believe you or to come over to your position? Imagine someone you know listening to you declare your position or opinion and then saying, "Oh, yeah? Prove it!" This is your audience — write to them. Ask yourself the following questions so that you will not be confronted with a person who says, "Prove it!"

- What evidence do I need to prove my idea to this skeptic?
- What would she or he disagree with me about?
- What does he or she share with me as common knowledge?
- What do I need to tell the reader?

Once a topic has been chosen, the purpose of the paper must be defined. Usually papers are written to explain, persuade, tell a story, or describe some object, experience, or theory.

If surfing is the topic of a paper, for example, you might explain what surfing is or how it is done. Likewise, you could try to persuade the reader to surf or not to surf. A story could be told of some famous or exceptional surfer, or else of an outstanding incident in your own surfing experience. A description of the experience of surfing is another possibility.

After defining the purpose of the paper, the thesis of the paper must be established. What end are you trying to achieve? Although the thesis might be obvious, it is still a good idea to summarize it in one sentence.

If the topic is fishing, for example, and the purpose is to explain what fishing is and how it is done, a thesis must now be established. Certainly, it is not just to write a collection of facts about fishing. This would be boring even to a fisherman. You should return to your interest in the topic. A conclusion is drawn or an observation made which links all the facts in the paper together. If fishing lowers a person's blood pressure because it relaxes them and they enjoy it, this could become the thesis of the paper.

Some examples of topics, purposes, and theses are given below.

Topic: Sewing
Purpose: To describe how it felt to sew my sister's wedding dress.
Thesis: Being able to sew made it possible for me to have an exciting
                experience.

Topic: Submarines.
Purpose: To explain how submarines work.
Thesis: Submarines work on very simple principles.

Topic: Summer camp
Purpose: To tell the story of an awful experience at summer camp.
Thesis: Summer camp is not always fun.

You should be in no rush to get to the typewriter. Inspiration alone is rarely the source of a good paper. If writing is the craft of expressing ideas, then you must have clear ideas to begin with. Take time to think and organize before going into a frenzy of writing.

Developing Organization for Your Topic

After deciding on a topic, you should think about its development. There are different patterns to use when organizing a research paper. Below are some common organizational patterns. You should try to match at least one of these patterns to your topic.

1. Chronological: Use this pattern to develop a topic according to when events take place. For example, with the topic of the development of drugs to treat AIDS, you could analyze and explain drug treatments that have been developed during the past decade, beginning with the earliest treatment, and ending with the most recent.

2. Compare and Contrast: Use this organizational pattern to show how aspects of a topic are the same and how they are different. For example, with the topic of

Chinese and Soviet Communism, you could write about Chinese government and then show how Soviet government was similar and how it differed.

3. Topical: Use this pattern to break the overall topic into fragments and analyze each fragment. For example, with the topic of Picasso's influence on modern art, one could discuss Cubism, his influence on sculpture, and his use of masks.

4. Problem-Solution: Use this organizational pattern to state a problem and analyze various solutions. You may also research and develop your own solution as long as it can be supported by research. For example, with the problem of homelessness in New York City, you could discuss solutions proposed by various homeless advocates and research what the government has done and is currently doing about the problem.

It is possible to use more than one pattern of organization for a research paper. Often a combination of these patterns is well suited to a particular topic. For instance, you could combine compare-contrast and chronological with the topic of Chinese and Soviet communism. You could compare both forms of Communism chronologically by showing how both forms of government differed and how they were the same in various periods of time.

Developing an Information Base for Your Topic

Once you have decided on a topic and have decided which organizational patterns you will use to develop it, you must further explore your topic. This is called developing an information base and it must be done before intensive research begins so that the research will be more focused. The procedure below explains how an information base is developed.

1. General Reading: You should keep in mind the organizational pattern(s) you chose and do some general reading on the topic. This reading should include an encyclopedia article plus any other pertinent information you have close at hand, such as a textbook.

2. Focused-Free Writing: Keeping the topic in mind, you must put pen to paper for at least ten uninterrupted minutes. During this time you should write continuously about any ideas you have regarding your chosen topic.

3. Who, What, Where, When, and Why?: You should use these words to list questions related to your topic. This might reveal part of a larger question that the research paper will attempt to answer.

4. List of Ideas, Questions, and Responses: You should make a list of any ideas, questions, and responses that come about when doing the above. This will help you develop a research plan. It is also possible that while listing these ideas, your topic becomes more focused and limited. Also, you might discover a way to use a different organizational pattern than you thought of previously.

Developing Your Thesis Statement

After selecting a topic, developing a pattern of organization for it, and developing an information base, you are ready to write a thesis statement. A thesis statement is one or two sentences conveying the main idea of the research paper and your aim in writing it. The entire research paper should revolve around the thesis statement; therefore, the research that you choose to use and the entire body of the paper should reflect back to the thesis statement. Since the thesis statement is the main idea holding the research paper together, it is crucial that it be well thought out. It is important to keep the thesis statement in mind while researching and, most importantly, while writing. You should keep your chosen organizational pattern in mind when composing your thesis statement.

A good thesis statement should define the topic of the research paper and state the aim of the paper, or what you are trying to achieve by writing about this particular topic. The thesis should also be related to the chosen pattern of organization. Below are some examples of thesis statements related to each of the five organizational patterns. These sample thesis statements are based on the model topics mentioned earlier.

1. Chronological: During the past decade, several AIDS drug treatments have been developed by pharmaceutical companies to treat HIV-infected individuals.

2. Topical: Pablo Picasso had a profound influence on modern art. His Cubist paintings, his sculpture, and his use of masks have each sparked major movements in the art world.

3. Compare and Contrast: Although China and the former Soviet Union were both Communist regimes with many of the same underlying principles, they also had many differences.

4. Problem-Solution: The number of homeless people in New York City is increasing while the scramble to find solutions to this problem continues.

A thesis statement can be either informative or persuasive in nature, depending upon the topic involved. An informative thesis is one that seeks to let the reader know all pertinent information about a particular subject and, if need be, explain that information. By contrast, a persuasive thesis is one wherein your goal is to persuade the reader on a matter of opinion. The focus of an informative thesis is the subject itself, while the focus of a persuasive thesis is the reader whom you want to influence. The aim of a persuasive thesis is to persuade and the aim of an informative thesis is to educate.

The introduction, body, and conclusion of a research paper all revolve around the thesis statement. It is of prime importance that every element in the paper somehow relate to the thesis. If any sentence or paragraph contained in the research paper does not relate to your thesis, then it is irrelevant and should be removed. Information that is unrelated to the thesis will only confuse the reader and weaken the strength of the paper. Your goal in composing your thesis will be lost to the reader if the reader must endure being exposed to irrelevant information.

After considering your topic and organizational pattern, and after preparing an information base, you should review all work done thus far. The following procedure should be helpful in forming a thesis statement.

1. Grouping Ideas: First, you should analyze your information base prepared earlier. You should look for ideas that are most interesting and group related ideas together.

2. Focused Free Writing: Keeping in mind the ideas that interest you most, you should write continuously for at least ten minutes. Afterward, you should read over your sentences, carefully searching for ones that can be developed into a thesis statement.

3. Questioning: You should make a list of questions by using your information base and your focused-free writing. You should then analyze your questions and notice if any are related. You should try to turn some of these questions into thesis statements.

4. Checking Thesis Statement: Lastly, you should check your thesis statement making sure that the statement mentions the topic of your paper and your aim in writing it. Also, your thesis must be able to be developed by research.

The thesis statement should be written and rewritten several times. These re-writes will ensure that your thesis is as near perfect as possible. Rewrites can be frustrating, but it is important that the thesis statement be the most well thought-out sentence in the entire research paper, considering that the entire paper revolves around it.

II. GATHERING MATERIAL

Writing a research paper is a long-term project; consequently, time must be scheduled during a term so that the completed paper can be delivered on time. Since the research paper must go through the same stages as any paper, use the stages of the writing process to plan time. Whatever time you have, a paper should be scheduled in such a manner that it can be completed by your professor's deadline.

Your research paper, although longer term, is basically another paper that must be written using the writing process. During the pre-writing stage, use the time you have to gather research at the library. Do not hesitate to seek the help of a research librarian in the library at your college. Research librarians can point out where to find the information sources you need.

An Overview of the Steps and Sources

Basically, you may find research material in either a card catalog or a computer catalog. Most libraries now have computer catalogs, so it is helpful to become computer literate to use them effectively. Sources that should be sought out in the library include, of course, books relevant to the topic that can be found in the Library of Congress subject headings or, in some libraries, in the Dewey Decimal System. These are the systems used to catalog information in most libraries. You must learn to use the systems to find what you need.

```
261 Alexander Library          --IRIS Library System - All * Choose Search


   What type of search do you wish to do?

      1. TIL - Title, journal title, series title, etc.

      2. AUT - Author, illustrator, editor, organization, etc.

      3. SUB - Subject heading assigned by library.

      4. NUM - Call number, ISBN, ISSN, etc.

      5. BOL - Boolean/Keyword search on title, author, and subject.

      6. LIM - Limit your search to a portion of the catalog.



   Enter number or code, then press enter <CR>; to exit type END:
```

Figure 1: An example of a main menu from a computer catalog.

In addition to books, you may use periodicals and journals that are relevant to the topic. The Reader's Guide to Periodical Literature and The New York Times Index are the two best sources for this information. Indexes for special disciplines such as psychology or medicine are available. Finally, various abstracting services are available to provide summaries of important recent articles and books relevant to a project.

After having discovered how to use these resources, you should develop a working bibliography, that is, a list on index cards of all the sources that might be used in the paper. You must be sure to include all the bibliographic information on one side of the cards (including author, title, publisher, city of publication, year of publication, and any other identifying information necessary). Put important notes on the other side of the cards, such as the author's thesis or main supporting evidence. You should do this in the beginning; so these notes will be available when you are writing the formal bibliography at the end.

Figure 2: Side One, sample card for working bibliography.

Thesis:	The beginning of life on Earth can be re-created in the laboratory by copying the environment of that time in the history of the Earth.
Of Importance:	Prehistoric Soup; Thermodynamics of life and living systems; and reassessing Earth's early atmosphere.

Figure 3: Side Two, sample card for working bibliography.

A research paper is a formal argument that will be judged on its thoroughness, its reasoning, and the supporting evidence for that reasoning. The research you conduct for your paper will provide the thoroughness and supporting evidence. You will find that once you have informed yourself about a topic, opinions and reasoning will follow. Working from this realization, a calculated, organized approach to your research cannot help but strengthen your research paper.

In researching sources for your research paper, bibliography cards will prove to be an invaluable tool for keeping track of your findings. Not only do they simplify the writing of the paper's final bibliography (when time can be precious), the cards are a handy form in which to access your working list of sources. With one item per card, you will later have multiple options for organizing your materials—chronologically, by form (books, periodicals, or other), or by the planned sequence of your paper.

General Reference Material

Often the simplest way to begin your research is to read about your subject in a general encyclopedia. This will introduce you to the areas you need to research, and give you a basis for a list of subjects and names to work from when you get to the card catalog. For the beginning, however, continue working in the reference section so that you can expand and refine your subject list. You will want to consult the "standard" initial sources first. From the general encyclopedias, your next step may vary with your research topic. If the subject of your paper is a specific person, consult the Who's Who texts, which range from the general to the specific. Many scientific subjects are covered individually in specialized encyclopedias and dictionaries. This is also true for some humanities and social science subjects. These specialized reference books will turn up when you go to the card catalog, so do not worry if you do not see one on your topic right away. They are also accessible from other reference books as you will see.

The following list gives a selection of common useful reference texts. The first two sections name the texts you should consult at this initial state of your research, and the second two sections list others for more advanced research, which will be discussed later:

Encyclopedia Britannica

Encyclopedia Americana

The Columbia Encyclopedia

The World Almanac

Who's Who, Who's Who in American Women, Who's Who in Religion,

Who Was Who in American Politics, etc.

Biography Index

Dictionary of American Biography

McGraw-Hill Encyclopedia of Science and Technology

Dictionary of Literary Terms

Oxford English Dictionary

Reader's Guide to Periodical Literature

The New York Times Index

Book Review Digest

Guide to Reference Books

First Step: The Master Index to Subject Encyclopedias

Register of Indexes

Books in Print

Facts on File

Arts and Humanities Citation Index

Science Citation Index

Social Sciences Citation Index

Card and Computer Catalogs

By now you know what key terms and names are relevant to your paper topic, and you can bring that knowledge to bear at the library's catalogs. Today, even local township libraries have computerized catalogs that allow you to enter a key word and get a list of related texts. As convenient as this seems, be sure to address the same subject with as many synonyms as you can think of, because the program's cross-referencing may not always be ideal. You should also supplement the computer's output by checking the card catalog. Sometimes certain references fall through the cracks between supposedly redundant catalogs. For the same reason, technology-haters should not forego consulting the computer catalog. Philosophies and therefore cataloguing priorities change from library to library.

```
 261 Alexander Library              --IRIS Library System - All * Choose Search


        For people, enter last name first.

            EX:   Bronte, Emily

            EX:   Mondrian, Piet

        For other authors, use normal word order.

            EX:   National Research Council

            EX:   Rutgers University



    Enter Author:                              Then press SEND
```

Figure 4: An example of the menu for a computer catalog search by author.

```
261 Alexander Library          --IRIS Library System - All * Choose Search


          Start at the beginning of the title and enter as many
          words of the title as you know below.

               EX:  Wuthering Heights

               EX:  How to Succeed in Business Without


    Enter title:                              Then press SEND
```

Figure 5: *An example of the menu for a computer catalog search by title.*

```
261 Alexander Library          --IRIS Library System - All * Choose Search


          Start at the beginning of the Library of Congress subject heading
          and enter as many words of the subject heading as you know below.
          Choose the most specific subject heading you can.

               EX:  molecular biology (NOT biology)

               EX:  feminism and literature (NOT literature)


    Enter subject:                            Then press SEND
```

Figure 6: *An example of the menu for a computer catalog search by subject.*

Another method of double-checking the cross-referencing of a catalog is to use all three of its bases for catalog entry. Each book is entered under its title, its author, and its subject. If a subject search produces a book that sounds like it will be useful in your term paper, look up the author to inspect his or her other works. This practice eliminates the chance of many cross-referencing omissions. Also, a title search should show you all editions of the text, allowing you to verify that you will be using the most recent edition. It is not unusual for prefaces to change with subsequent editions, so do not automatically discount earlier editions—you may find useful quotes in the earlier prefaces.

Remember that the library's catalog only lists the information available in that particular library or library network. As you find useful texts and articles, consult their bibliographies for additional sources. You may find these additional texts at other libraries, be able to borrow them from an instructor, or purchase them. The main point is that these additional sources are easier to find when you know exactly what to ask for.

Indexes for Periodicals and Other Materials

The usefulness of periodicals varies widely from topic to topic, but they should always be consulted. You would be amazed to learn how specific and bizarre some magazine titles are. Note that you will not find periodicals listed in the card catalog. The ultimate authority on periodicals is The Reader's Guide to Periodical Literature, a series of hard-cover volumes, usually green or brown, spanning the past several decades. Each volume covers a year, except the most recent soft-cover volumes, which cover quarters of the current year, and older volumes, which may cover spans of years. Unfortunately, you must repeat your topic scan from volume to volume, but the Reader's Guide is very precise and as you become familiar with its format you will find your information more quickly. Because it is a comprehensive index, the Reader's Guide will list magazines that your library does not have, but you should still record these in your notes. Different libraries have different periodical banks, and later research may compel you to expand your search to other nearby libraries.

SURFACES

See also

Interfaces

Thin films

Areas and volumes

The crystalline face of soap films [work of Jean E. Taylor]
I. Peterson. il *Science News* 134:135 Ag 27 '88

Geometry for segregating polymers [copolymers; work of Edwin
L. Thomas and David Hoffman] I. Peterson. il *Science
News* 134:151 S 3 '88

SURFACTANTS *See* Surface active substances

SURFING

See also

Boardsailing

Bodyboarding

Ice surfing

Davey's little surfer girl [A. Johnson] J. Lieber. il pors *Sports
Illustrated* 69:48+ Jl 25 '88

In your face, Spuds Mackenzie! Rocky, the beach-blanket
bowwow, hangs twenty with ease [surfing dog] il *People
Weekly* 30:66 O 17 '88

The mechanics of waves–and the art of surfing. R. Woikome
il *Oceans* 21:36-41 My/Je '88

Of surf and science [surfing stellar sea lions off coast of
Vancouver Island] W.M. Roberts. il *Sea Frontiers* 34:48
N/D '88

Surf report: tune into the wavelength. il *'Teen* 32:26 Je
'88

Equipment

See also

Quicksilver, Inc.

Photographs and photography

Super surf shooters. P. Skinner. il *Peterson's Photographer
Magazine* 17:16-20+ Ag '88

SURGEON-GENERAL'S OFFICE (U.S.) *See* United States
Surgeon General's Office

SURGEONS

See also

Kinal, Murl E.

The best way to find a plastic surgeon. R. Sandroff. il *Working
Woman* 13:121-2 My '88

How to check out a surgeon. L. Kleinmann. *Health (New
York, N.Y.)* 20:8 Ag '88

Looking for "Doctor Right" [plastic surgeon] J. Schmid. *Vogue*
178:206+ Ja '88

Sports

The whole athlete [plastic surgeon J. Emery] J. Popper. il
Esquire 109:71-2 Mr '88

SURGEONS AS AUTHORS

This pen and the scalpel. R. Selzer. il por *The New York
Times Magazine* p30-1 Ag 21 '88

SURGERY

Figure 7: Example of a listing from The Reader's Guide to Periodical Literature.

For information that would have been "news" at some point, consult The New York Times Index. These volumes, usually red, are organized much like The Reader's Guide to Periodical Literature. Most libraries have the past several decades of The New York Times on microfiche, so these articles will almost always be available. The Sunday New York Times has a magazine section that contains a reputable book review column. These reviews are listed in the Book Review Digest, a separate index. The column's coverage is not limited to bestsellers and novels, and often includes scholarly texts and reference books; therefore, any subject is worth looking for in the Book Review Digest. Again, those reviews will most often be found on microfiche within that Sunday's New York Times.

SUPREME COURTS (STATE). See also
Death, D 18
New York State – Elections – Courts, D 23
SURFING
  Article discusses career of surfer Mark Foo, who drowned while surfing Pillar Point in California; photo; map (M). D 29,B,14:1
SURGEON GENERAL (US). See also
Public Health Service, D 18
SURGERY and SURGEONS. See also
Heart, D 21
SURVEILLANCE SYSTEMS. Use Security and
Warning Systems
SURVEYS AND SERIES. See also
Agriculture, D 28
Bombs and Bomb Plots, D 18
Crime and Criminals, D 25,26,28,29,30
Medicine and Health, D 18
Parks and Other Recreation Areas, D 26
Rwanda, D 29
United States – Congress (US), D 20
United States Armament and Defense, D 30
United States Politics and Government, D 17

Figure 8: An example of listings from The New York Times Index.

Other valuable research tools are guides, indexes, and registers to reference books. The merit of First Step: The Master Index to Subject Encyclopedias is evident in the title. Such a text would be able to lead you directly to something as specific as the five-volume Grzimek's Encyclopedia of Mammals. You should also consult the Guide to Reference Books and the Register of Indexes and Books in Print. For an example of a listing by subject, see Figure 9.

A profoundly useful form of reference is the Citation Index. When you find a text, an essay, an article, or a report that addresses the subject you are researching, you should bring its bibliographical data to either the Arts and Literature Citation Index, the Science Citation Index, or the Social Science Citation Index (all published by the Institute for Scientific Information). If your library does not have them, find one that does. These indexes allow you to look up an article (by the author's name, then the title) and see a list of subsequent articles that have made reference to it and cited the article in their bibliographies. This gives you the opportunity to read the author's peers' published responses to his or her discovery, theory, argument, or proposal. You tap into a professional dialog on the subject you are researching. These responses give you the material to evaluate and defend your sources. The Citation Indexes also give an authors' sources index that lists all texts cited by an author in the bibliographies of his or her various publications. There are also subject indexes with which you might access a Citation Index directly.

```
SURFACANTS
see Surface Active Agents
SURFBOARD RIDING
see Surfing
SURFING
see also Windsurfing
Ambrose, Greg. A Surfer's Guide to Hawaii. LC 91-70850.
    (Illus.). 160p. 1991. pap. 10.96 (0-0935848-90-8) Ness Pr.
Ball, Dic. California Surfriders. 1946. 2nd ed. 116p. 1946
    cloth 19.95 (0-911449-05-1) Mountain Sea.
Bruce, Jill B. Surf Lifesavers of Australia. (illus.). 64p. 1993
    12.95 (0-86417-480-2, pub. by Kangaroo Pr ) Seven
    Hills Bk Dists.
Carroll, Nick, ed. The next Wave: the World of Surfing.
    (Illus.). 240p. 1991. 29.98 (1-55859-162-1) Abbeville Pr.
Doudt, Kenny Surfing with the Great White Shark. LC 92-
    90967. (orig.). (YA) Date not set.pap. 8.95
    (0-9633342-7-1) Shark-Bite.
Jenkins, Bruce. North Shore Chronicles: Big Wave Surfing in
    Hawaii. (Illus.). 208p. (Orig). 1991.pap.12.95
    (1-55643-105-8) North Atlantic.
Noll, Greg & Gabbard, Andrea. Da Bull: Life over the Edge.
    (Illus.).200p. 1992pap. 16.95 (1-55643-143-0) North
    Atlantic.
Orbelian, Geroge. Essentialk Surfing 3rd ed. (Illus.). 247p.
    1987. pap. 9.95 (0-9610548-2-4) Orbelian Arts.
Pfeiffer, C. Boyd. The Complete Surfcaster. (Illus.). 247p.
    198. pap. 14.95 (1-55821-052-0) Lyons & Burford.
*Renneker, Mark. Sick Surfers Ask the SurDocs & Dr.
    Geofd. 1993. pap. 12.95 (0-923521-26-7) Bull pub.
Stem, David & Cleary, Bill. Surfing Guide to Southern
    California. LC 63-17835. 256p. 1977. 8.95
    (0-911449-06-X) Mountain Sea.
VanDyke, Fred. Surfing Huge Wave with Ease. 64p. 1992.
    pap. 8.95 (1-56647-008-0) Mutual Pub H1.
Wardlaw, Lee. Cowabunga! The Complete Book of Surfing.
    168p. 1991. pap. 9.95 (0-380-75996-9), Camelot) Avon.
```

Figure 9: An example of a listing in Books in Print by subject.

Bibliography Cards

In conducting this research, you must make bibliography cards to keep track of all of your potential sources. Using one card per text or article, note the author's name, the title of the work, its place of publication, its publisher, and its year of publication.

A special note should be made about the style of presenting titles of books, magazines, newspapers, and plays. While it is correct to either italicize or under-line these titles, it is preferred to underline them because some computer printers have indistinct italics characters, or none at all. Specific formats and variants are handled as follows:

One-Author Books

Note that the author is given last name first; the full author's name is fol-lowed by a period, and then the title; the title is underlined and ends with a pe-riod; the city is stated, followed by a colon and the publisher's name; next is a comma, the year of publication, and finally a period (see Figure 10).

Newman, Art. The Illustrated Treasury of Medical Curiosa. New York: McGraw-Hill, Inc. 1988.

Figure 10: Sample bibliography card for a one-author book.

Two-Author Books

Note that the authors are in the order that they appear on the title page (not necessarily alphabetical order), and that the second name is given first name first.

Colson, Charles and Jack Eckerd. Why America Doesn't Work. Dallas: Word Publishing, 1991.

Multiple-Author Books

If the book has more than three authors, the name that occurs first alpha-betically is chosen to represent the group, "et al" meaning "and others."

> Adams, Raymond F., et al. <u>The Book of the American West</u>. New York: Simon & Schuster, 1963.

One-Editor Books

Note that the title of the editor, given as "ed.," follows the name after a comma. The period abbreviating "editor" and the other preceding the title merge into one.

> Booss, Claire, ed. <u>A Treasury of Irish Myth, Legend, and Folklore</u>. New York: Gramercy Books, 1986.

Note that variants for edited books change in the same pattern as authored books.

One-Translator Books

Note that translations are distinct works that can vary widely with mutual sources. List the author's name first, and place the translator's name after the book's title. Precede the translator's name with *Trans*. For example:

> Chaucer, Geoffrey. <u>The Canterbury Tales</u>. Trans. R.M. Lumiansky. New York: Simon and Schuster Inc., 1954.

Note that variants for translator books change in the same pattern as authored books.

Compilation Books or Anthologies

In these, chapters are written individually by separate authors, generating the equivalent of an article. The article is the true reference, not the book as a whole, so the author of the article is more relevant than the editor of the book. The format is almost the same except for adding the article author and title to the beginning, and article titles are put in quotes rather than underlined. Add the editor's name, first name first, after the title of the book (see Figure 11).

Christianson, John, "Lahaina Whale-Song." An Anthology of
Polynesian Poetry and Song. Ed. Ronald Jarret.
Toronto: University of Toronto Press, 1982.

Figure 11: Sample bibliography card for a compilation book or anthology.

Note that variants for articles in compilation books or anthologies change in the same pattern as authored books.

Periodicals

Note that periodical references take a form similar to compilation books, but omit the editors and the city of publication. Also note the addition of the volume number and more specified date of publication (see Figure 12).

Colley, Linda. "Women and their Political Power." The
Wilson Quarterly, vol. XVI (Spring 1992): 31-36.

Figure 12: Sample bibliography card for a periodical.

Note that variants for articles in periodicals change in the same pattern as authored books.

Encyclopedia Articles

Note that encyclopedia references are similar to periodical references, but that they further omit the name of the publisher. Also, the edition number is added after the encyclopedia name and before the year. Many encyclopedia articles are written anonymously, and so are alphabetized by the article title. For an authored encyclopedia title, include the author's name as for a periodical (see Figure 13).

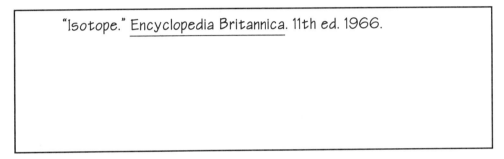

Figure 13: Sample bibliography card for an encyclopedia article.

Finding Usable Information

Now that you have a stack of bibliography cards of potential sources, you will find and evaluate these sources. For books, first skim the preface and table of contents to see if it truly deals with your topic. Then, the most helpful check is to look up your topic in the book's index to see how many pages are listed. The more continuous pages listed, the more informative those passages will be. Remember to use various synonyms for your topics to insure that you find all your needed information. Articles usually require skimming for evaluation, but some more scholarly journals will have indexes to check. At this hands-on stage you will have the opportunity to see how recent the edition is, and to examine the credentials of the author(s). If you find that you have bibliography cards for which you cannot find the books, keep them in case you later have access to a different library or other facility.

Notecards

Notecards are the best way to keep track of the information you find, and they will be handy as you organize and write your paper. Write a few words across the top of the card identifying its contents. In the body of the card, write the idea, information, or quotation (see Figure 14). Be sure to put only one item on each card, because two bits of information found on the same page in a source text may ultimately be on two distant pages of your research paper. Make it clear whether you are quoting directly from your source, or paraphrasing the author's words. If you are quoting, you will have to be sure and make this clear when you use the quote in your research paper, and it's best to mark this in your notes so that you do not inadvertently use the author's own words without acknowledging it. At the bottom of the card, record the author's name, the text's title, and the specific page number(s) of whatever inspired your note. This will refer you to the bibliography card that has the rest of the required citation information.

Water Waves

"... water particles move in a nearly circular path, its motion having both transverse and logitudinal components."

Tipler, Physics p. 399

Figure 14: Sample notecard.

III. WRITING THE PAPER

Putting Your Notes Into an Outline

Making an outline is the next logical step in preparing a paper. It requires only a short time to prepare, and it helps tremendously when actually writing the paper. Writing a paper without an outline is like taking a walk through a strange city without a map. The destination might be reached, but only by chance. With a map, the traveler can know the way in advance. Similarly, an outline is a plan; it will guide you through the paper by clear and logical steps.

When writing an outline, you should note all thoughts on the topic in short phrases, considering whether they contribute to the purpose and point of the paper. To return to the surfing example, you might want to explain what surfing is and why it is enjoyable. The following thoughts might occur:

> surfing is fun
> you need a board
> what the board is made of
> length and weight of the board
> how to learn
> where surfing came from
> you can surf on Long Island, but it is better in Hawaii

The next step is organization. First, group the ideas. Many entries concern the board. Group them under a main heading called The Board. Then four other points remain: surfing is fun, learning to surf, history of surfing, and good places to surf. Along with The Board, these become the main points, because they cannot be grouped under any other heading. These are the major headings; all other points will fall under one of them.

These main points must be organized. The order must be logical to both you and the reader. They should develop, or work toward, an end.

The following is a sample outline for the surfing paper:

Introduction
History of surfing
The board
     why you need it
     its length and weight
     what it is made of
How to learn to surf
Surfing is fun
Best places to surf

Now, in looking over the outline, you might decide to spend the major part of the paper discussing the board and how to learn and might make the last two sections rather short. Or, you might decide to make all the sections about the same length, except the first one, which should be relatively short because it is a general introduction to the paper. Decisions of this nature should be made before any writing is attempted.

This outline will become even more important later on because it will be presented in your final draft. The outline is placed after the title page and table of contents. This outline will be the same one that you used for this prewriting stage.

Your outline should be structured in a precise manner. An outline is a chart of subjects, branching from the general to the increasingly specific. The broadest topics are indicated with upper case roman numerals and begin at the left margins. The largest subtopics of these are placed beneath them, indented five spaces and sequenced by upper case letters. Subtopics of subtopics become increasingly narrow, continuing from subjects that are numbered with Arabic numerals, to those followed by lower case letters and finally to lower case roman numerals, each indented an additional five spaces from the left margin. Roman numerals are given extra indentation to give equally-ranked topics the same starting point at the left. Each numeral and letter marking is followed by a period and two spaces. The following fictitious biography outline demonstrates the outline format:

> I. Childhood
>   A. Parentage
>   B. War Years
>   1. hardships
>   a. poverty
>   b. family
>   i. brother enlists, dies
>   ii. parents die in bombing
>   iii. siblings distributed
>   2. early accomplishments
> II. Adulthood
>   A. Writing Career
>   1. early struggle
>   2. success
>   a. first recognition
>   b. rise to fame
>   3. later works
>   B. Family
>   1. Marriage
>   2. Offspring
>   C. Death

Each topic should have either zero, two or more subtopics. Never give an "A/a" without a "B/b" or an "I/1/i" without a "II/2/ii." When you find that you have six or more subtopics of equal rank under the same topic, stop to consider whether they should be under two different topics. Note that only the two highest subtopic rankings are capitalized, and that no level of the outline is more than a sentence fragment.

The Structure of a Research Paper

Before any writing begins, it is important that you understand how a research paper should be structured. A research paper consists of three parts: the introduction, the body, and the conclusion. Each of these parts is related and the way that they are related is through the thesis statement. This is because all elements of a research paper must point to the thesis statement. This is crucial in order to write a coherent, well-constructed research paper.

The introduction generally consists of one to two paragraphs. It introduces readers to the topic of the research paper and prepares them for what lies ahead in the body of the paper. An introduction should point to what the paper is about and then end with the thesis statement, which is what you are trying to accomplish in your paper. Several different devices can be used to lead into the thesis statement. They are as follows:

1. Give background information.
2. Use of a quotation.
3. An anecdote or story of interest.
4. Use of statistics.
5. Make an analogy.
6. Ask a question.

After you make a statement of your thesis, you can begin the body of your paper, where most of your research will be contained. Support of the thesis is made in the body of a research paper. Generally, at least three main ideas or reasons should be made in the body to support the thesis well. No mention should be made of any points that are unrelated to the thesis statement because this will only confuse the reader by distorting the paper.

In an informative paper, where you are trying to educate the reader, there should be at least three items of data about a topic mentioned in the thesis statement. The data should be from academic research and should be cited as such. For a persuasive paper, you are attempting to sway the reader on a matter of opinion. A good way to do this is to mention a conflicting opinion only once early on in the paper and then refute it with at least three valid reasons of your own as to why your view is the right one. These reasons must, of course, be supported by research documented in the body of the paper.

For all research papers, whether they be persuasive or informative, the ideas or reasons in the body should be presented in order of least important to most important. This strategy makes the strength of the paper keep building. Perhaps most importantly, this strategy will keep the reader interested throughout the paper. If you make your strongest point first and follow with weaker points, then the reader will lose interest after the first point. The body of the paper is where most of your research is contained.

Transitions are an important tool to use throughout a research paper, but they are of prime importance in the body of a paper. Transitions serve to ease the reader's journey from idea to idea. By using transitions and transitional phrases correctly, you will be able to write a more smooth, polished research paper. The right transition can refine a good paper into an excellent one. See Appendix B for suggested transitions.

The final part of a research paper is the conclusion, which is generally one to two paragraphs long. Its purpose is to bring the discussion of a paper to its logical end. Ideas mentioned in the body of the paper should be reinforced in the conclusion. The conclusion should flow gracefully and not be so abrupt as to leave readers with a sense of being cut off. You can use the same devices for the conclusion that were mentioned previously for the introduction of the paper. You may also use any of the following for the conclusion:

1. Summarize main points of paper.
2. Refer to the future.
3. State a call for action or awareness.

Revising and Rewrites

Now that you have an outline and know how a research paper is structured, you can begin writing. You should expect to have to rewrite your paper several times, so you should plan for this. With each revision, your paper will become clearer and better written. The following is a suggested procedure for revising research papers:

1. First Draft: Following your outline, you should begin forming complete sentences to connect ideas from the outline. Transitional words are helpful in accomplishing this (refer to Appendix B for words and phrases to use in transitions). To maintain organization, you should make note in the draft document of the numbers on notecards that correspond to specific sources. This is important for footnoting later. At this point the aim is not perfection, so spelling, grammar, and punctuation are not important. If possible, it is best to begin writing at the word processor, however, if you prefer to hand-write a first draft, you should double space it and leave large margins. This will make revising much easier. It will probably take you several writing sessions just to complete a first draft.

2. Second Draft: You should perfect your paper in the second draft, however, this is still not the time to correct grammar, spelling, and punctuation. You should focus on each section and the strength of it. You should also focus on making sure that the sections are well linked with transitions. Some sections may not need to be revised, but most will. Some might require minor rewriting, while others might need to be rewritten several times. It is usually helpful to wait a day or two between drafts. You will be able to gain better objectivity by stepping away from your paper for a couple of days. If a particular section seems weak or unclear to the writer, then it will be even more unclear to your audience, the reader. Any sections that seem weak to you should definitely be reworked.

3. Third Draft: Now is the time for you to correct surface features such as spelling, grammar, and punctuation. This is the editing phase of revising. When editing, it is helpful to read aloud slowly and carefully. You will have to do this several times to catch all errors, however, nothing is as good as having someone else read the paper, so if a friend is available, you should ask him or her to read through the paper. Waiting several hours between editing sessions will make your efforts more effective. While editing, it is helpful for you to have a dictionary, thesaurus, and grammar book by your side. The reason that editing is considered the last step in successful rewriting is that paying attention to surface features too soon can hamper the flow of ideas when writing. Once you feel certain that you have corrected all errors, asking a friend to read over the paper can be a good way to catch every last error.

4. <u>Additional Drafts</u>: You should keep rewriting the paper until you are satisfied with it. This might mean writing some additional drafts. The higher your standards are for your paper the more likely your grade will be higher. Once you are satisfied with your paper, you are ready to compose a final draft which should include footnotes.

The Footnote

Footnotes acknowledge your sources of information while establishing the credibility of your materials. Failure to acknowledge sources is a crime called plagiarism, which is grounds for failure in all classrooms and expulsion at most colleges. A footnote should accompany every direct quotation, give the source of any important piece of information, and designate opinions borrowed from other writers. Another use of footnotes is to give longer parenthetic comments without interrupting the flow of the paper. These may include definitions or explanations that some readers would need and others would not. Also, if you cannot resist a tangent, placing it in a footnote may preserve the organizational integrity of your paper as a whole.

To indicate a footnote within the body of your paper, use a raised number—a superscript on a word processor, or a regular number placed at a half-line up from the rest of the text on a typewriter. Footnotes are numbered continuously from "1" up throughout the paper. The number should be placed at the end of a quotation outside the quotation marks, at the end of a paraphrased sentence, at the end of a paraphrased paragraph, or at the end of a word or phrase requiring an explanation or sparking a tangent handled in a footnote.

There are two choices for the location of your footnotes. The first is at the bottom of the page within the margins (as shown below)[1]. The second choice (which most professors prefer) has all footnotes at the end of the paper and not on each page.

If you are going to place your footnotes at the bottom of the page and you are using a typewriter, make four or more erasable marks at half-inch intervals along the side of your paper starting at the top of the bottom margin. Keep track of how many footnote numbers occur on each page and use one mark for each note. This is just a guide — some notes will be longer than others. Separate the last line of text for that page from the footnotes with seven underscores starting from the left margin on the very next line. Then skip a line and begin your notes. Footnotes are typed single-spaced with no lines skipped between notes.

The content of a footnote that denotes credit for a source of information or wisdom is somewhat similar to a bibliography entry, but bears an important difference. A footnote citing must accurately and specifically tell the page or pages within a source where the words or ideas are found. If your paper is properly footnoted, a reader should be able to find the source of a credited quote in a library without consulting the paper's bibliography.

Quotations and paraphrases are footnoted with the author's name, the title, and the exact page numbers of the material. All footnotes are indented three spaces and begin with the footnote number followed by a period and two spaces. Specific formats and variants are handled as follows:

_____

1. William Shakespeare, <u>A Midsummer Night's Dream</u> (New York: Washington Square Press, 1993) 102.

One-Author Books

The author's name is followed by a comma, the title of the text underlined, the publishing data in parenthesis, the page numbers, and finally a period.

      1. J.D. Salinger, The Catcher in the Rye (Boston: Little, Brown Books, 1945) 100-101.

      2. George Orwell, Animal Farm (New York: Harcourt, Brace, Jovanovich, Inc., 1946) 205.

Note the single spacing, no skipped lines and that author's name occurs first name first. Also, note that page numbers are not preceded by any letters or words.

Two-Author and Multiple-Author Books

Because footnotes give the first name first for all authors' names, plural author texts do not have a significant variation. They are handled as follows:

      3. Chuck Colson and Jack Eckerd, Why America Doesn't Work (Dallas: Word Publishing, 1991) 60-62.

      4. Ramon Adams, et al., The Book of the American West (New York: Simon & Schuster, 1963) 62.

Note that unnamed authors are denoted with the Latin "et al."

One-Editor and One-Translator Books

Be sure to make the distinction between authors and editors and translators. The format remains constant, as follows:

      5. Claire Booss, ed., A Treasury of Irish Myth, Legend and Folklore (New York: Gramercy Books, 1986) 304-305.

    6. Frank O. Copley, trans., <u>Cicero: On Old Age and On Friendship</u> (New York: John Wiley & Sons, Inc., 1963) 112.

Note that the title format for the translated texts also carries over from the one-author footnote rules. Variants for these types of footnotes follow the same pattern as one-author books.

Compilation Books or Anthologies

We are required to distinguish when chapters are authored individually. The editor's name will be inserted between the book title and the publishing information as follows:

    7. Janet Adelman, "Male Bonding in Shakespeare's Characters," <u>Shakespeare's Rough Magic</u> eds. Peter Ericson and Coppella Kahn (New York: Dodd, 1971) 73

Longer footnotes such as these require one to be wary when using a typewriter. Variants for these types of footnotes follow the same pattern as one-author books.

Periodicals and Encyclopedia Articles

Simple author and title references, even with the addition of editors and greater titles, will not suffice for these footnotes. Because of the nature of the sources, both require volume numbers to be cited, as follows:

    8. Linda Colley, "Women and Their Political Power," <u>The Wilson Quarterly</u>, vol. XVI: 20-21.

    9. "Isotope," <u>Encyclopedia Britannica</u>, 1985 ed., 311-312.

The edition reference for encyclopedias in footnotes is very important to insure the accuracy of the page numbers.

Special Citations

Biblical, dramatic, and poetic footnote citations have special convenient forms for brevity and clarity. These will probably look familiar:

 10. John 19:6.
 11. William Shakespeare, <u>Othello</u>, V.ii.1-6.
 12. William Wordsworth, "The World is Too Much With Us," ll.11-12. See <u>The Norton Anthology of Poetry</u>, Third edition, shorter.

The Bible format is so standard that <u>The Bible</u> is not mentioned by name, but we give the book, chapter, and verse. For plays, the author and title are followed by a series of numbers. The upper case roman numerals tell the act; the lower case numerals tell the scene within the act; and the Arabic numerals tell the lines within the scene. For poetry, we give the author, the title, and the line numbers preceded by "l." or "ll." for "line" or "lines." Poetry considered classic literature is not associated with a single text, but to be polite we give the source we used by title and edition.

Another special citation is quoting text second hand. At times, an original work is unavailable or of limited necessity. A second work that quotes the first may be used as a source for that first work, as follows:

 13. William Butler Yeats, <u>Fairy and Folk Tales of the Irish Peasantry,</u> quoted in Claire Booss, ed., <u>A Treasury of Irish Myth, Legend, and Folklore</u> (New York: Gramercy Books, 1986), vii-ix.

It may seem easier to claim the Yeats text as a direct source, but remember that a reader is meant to be able to refer to your sources. The secondary source is what is available to you and must be recognized.

Repeat Footnotes

Abbreviated formats exist for second and subsequent citations of the same text. For example:

14. Salinger, 100-101.
15. Salinger, 100-101.
16. Adelman, 74-75.
17. Adelman, 78.

Here we referenced J.D. Salinger's The Catcher in the Rye pages 100-101 from footnote 1, and then referenced the same pages a third time in footnote 14. Then we referenced Janet Adelman's "Male Bonding..." article from footnote 7, but for different pages. The last reference cites a new page of Adelman's article.

If you have used two books by the same author and need to footnote both of them, the repeat footnotes will have the author's last name and a shortened form of the title of the work. For example:

18. Orwell, Animal 87.
19. Orwell, 1984 22-26.

Here we referenced George Orwell's Animal Farm page 87 from footnote 2, and then we referenced another book by Orwell, 1984 pages 22-26.

Quotations and the Appendix

The format for quoting within the body of your paper varies with the length and nature of the quote. For a standard quoted sentence, put it in quotes and begin with a capital letter. For sentence fragments, use quotes, begin with a lower case letter, and maintain grammatical flow between your text and the quoted text. Text quotations longer than two lines should be introduced with a colon:

...and begin on the next line indented five spaces (the same as the beginning of a paragraph) and be single-spaced. The last line should end with the footnote number, just like the end of any quote."[22]

At the end of such a quote, resume double spacing and begin the next sentence at the left margin to continue the paragraph. Note that a quote (especially an indented one) should almost never end a paragraph, because if it deserves quotation it deserves your comments.

When quoting lines of poetry or verse drama, indicate the break from line to line with a "/," such as "Look out stomach,/Here it comes!" For multiple lines, set the quotation apart like a longer text quotation by indenting and single spacing, such as:

> It is the cause, it is the cause, my soul.
> Let me not name it to you, you chaste stars.
> It is the cause. Yet I'll not shed her blood
> Nor scar that whiter skin of hers than snow,
> And smooth as monumental alabaster.
> Yet she must die, else she'll betray more men.[22]

Some may prefer to include the line numbers noted at five- or ten-line intervals for greater understanding when subsequently referring to parts of the quoted verse. These line numbers should be taken from the source, not counted as the lines occur out of context in your paper.

Any quotation that seems extremely long or repeatedly referred to may be better placed as an appendix. Footnotes for a quoted section may read "14. See Appendix A." as long as in addition to providing the passage the appendix cites the source. Other uses of appendices are to provide statistical tables and charts that support data in the paper but that do not need to be read in the continuity of the body of the paper; and to relocate longer explanatory footnotes for a neater looking body. Appendices should occur between the body of the paper and its bibliography. They should be labeled with capital letters, such as "Appendix B." This title should occur centered at the top line of the first page of the appendix.

The Basics of the Bibliography

Your paper will end with a bibliography labeled "BIBLIOGRAPHY" centered at the top line of the page. Skipping two lines, enter your single-spaced source references with one space skipped between each reference. The format for these references is exactly as described for the bibliography cards. The references should be alphabetized based upon the first word, unless an uncredited title begins with "The," "An," or "A," in which case refer to the second word. Include any source that contributed to the paper, increasing your understanding of the subject, even if the source was never quoted or paraphrased. You may decide to classify the entries to your bibliography by book, periodical, and other types of source. Another practice is to distinguish between primary readings and secondary readings. Any such classifications should be labeled and internally alphabetized.

The Title Page

The research paper's first sheet should be the title page. Note that this is not a cover page—illustrations and pictures are unnecessary and inappropriate. One third of the page from the top, center the title of your paper using standard book title capitalization. For longer titles, double-space between lines, continue to center the lines, and distribute the words to create lines of nearly equal length. You may also apply these rules to make two lines of a longer one-line title. At the bottom-right corner of the page, observing the 1-inch margins, place a single-spaced block that gives your name on the first line, the course for which the paper is required on the next one or two lines, the teacher's name on the following line, and the date on the last line (1 inch from the bottom of the page). The longest entry should dictate the starting point for the others such that all are lined up on their left side, as such:

Your Name

The Course

The Teacher

Date

The date should be given in the format of the month as a word, followed by the day of the month given as a number with a comma, and finally the year as a number, such as July 4, 1776. The date you give should generally be the due date, even when you submit your paper early (this assists identification of the assignment). If circumstances require you to submit your paper late, clarity and honesty dictate that the date on the paper should be the actual date of submission.

Preparing Your Paper for Presentation—Typing and Proofreading

Standardized presentation formats primarily serve to emphasize the content of research papers. When margins and citation methods are universal from paper to paper, the grader is free to examine the material being presented. Standardization of abbreviations and other shortcuts provide clarity and convenience to both writer and grader without potentially confusing explanatory keys. The assignment of a research paper is meant to test your research and reasoning, which is where all your efforts have been concentrated. Do not allow carelessness in your presentation detract from these greater labors.

Your research paper should be typed on 8-1/2 × 11 inch white paper. The paper should be of good quality, with some cotton or "rag" content for thickness. This thickness will prevent blank spaces of a page from revealing the contents of the next page, which is considered distracting even when it is too faint to read. If you are using continuous-feed paper, as many printers accept, avoid paper with distinct perforation points; most quality continuous-feed papers feature fine perforation. It is increasingly rare for papers to be accepted handwritten. Never submit a handwritten paper without explicitly being given permission to do so. Even with such permission, a typed paper is always preferable if at all possible. If you are handwriting your paper, use college-ruled lined paper and print as opposed to using script. All rules for presentation format will apply equally to a handwritten paper.

The margins of your paper should be 1 inch for the top, bottom, and right. The left margin will be 1-1/4 inches. The page numbers will be in the top margin, located at the top-right margin two rows of type above the first line of the page. The first page of each chapter will be an exception to this format in two respects: the top margin will be 3 inches, and there will be no page number given. Note that footnotes, if they are placed on the same page as the reference, do not occupy the bottom margin. They obey all margins and must be planned for. In most cases it is acceptable and even preferred to bind the pages of your research paper with a single staple in the top left corner. Some graders and/or students may prefer to use a cover with a left-edge binder. When such binders are used, the left margin of the paper should be 1-1/2 inches while all other margins and rules remain unchanged.

Paper Size = 8-1/2 x 11

Paper Weight = twenty pound or better

Paper Color = white

Margins
  Top = 1 inch. 3 inches for the first page of
    each chapter or section

  Bottom = 1 inch

  Right = 1 inch

  Left = 1-1/4 inch. 1-1/2 if your paper is to be bound.

Spacing = doubled

Page Numbering = At the top-right margin, two rows
    above the first line. No page number
    on the first page.

Figure 15: Reference Table for Presentation of Paper.

Now your paper is complete. Proofread it again and have another person also proofread it. Verify that all of your sources are in your bibliography, especially those cited in your footnotes. Be sure you have included a table of contents and your outline. Erase any pencil lines you may have drawn to guide your margins or footnote placement. Make sure the pages are all present, in order and right side up. In other words, assume nothing — examine your paper with the clear mind that your grader will have. When you are confident that the paper has reached the status of "final draft," bind and submit it.

HELPFUL HINTS ON GRAMMAR AND WRITING

I. SENTENCE ERRORS

Dangling Modifiers

The dangling modifier is the most bizarre and comical of all sentence errors. Because it is such a glaring error, it stops readers dead in their tracks. The sentence lacks clarity, and the reader must take a moment to determine the writer's intention. The most common kind of dangling modifier is the dangling participle.

NO: At age six, my father taught me to swim.
YES: When I was six, my father taught me to swim.

NO: After showing the experiment, it was time to go home.
YES: After he showed us the experiment, we had to go home.

NO: The door was shut while dancing with Debbie.
YES: The door was shut while I was dancing with Debbie.

The difficulty with the sentences above is that the reader is not sure who is doing what. *"The door was shut while dancing with Debbie"* is ambiguous. *Who* is dancing with Debbie? The door? It is important to be clear about the sense of every sentence. Meaning can be completely changed when a word or phrase is moved into or out of the proper place.

Modifiers (participles, infinitives, and gerunds—verbals) usually dangle because, as in some of the examples above, the verbal is in search of a subject to modify.

Misplaced Modifiers

There are other types of modifiers that cause confusion when they are out of place. It is not important to learn the names of the various errors one could make, but it is important to avoid such errors. In general, structure a sentence logically by placing the modifier near the word it modifies. In each of the following examples, a phrase is out of place.

NO:	I saw two stores and a movie theater walking down the street.
YES:	Walking down the street, I saw two stores and a movie theater.
NO:	Harold watched the painter gaping in astonishment.
YES:	Harold watched the painter and gaped in astonishment.
	Gaping in astonishment, Harold watch the painter.
NO:	You can see the moon standing in the front yard.
YES:	If you stand in the front yard, you can see the moon.
	Standing in the front yard, you can see the moon.

There are some words that must always be placed immediately before the word they modify, or they will cause confusion. These are words like *almost, only, just, even, hardly, nearly, not,* and *merely.*

NO:	Jane almost polished the plate until it shined.
YES:	Jane polished the plate until it almost shined.
NO:	The store on the corner only sells that toaster.
YES:	Only the store on the corner sells that toaster.

Look at how the meaning can change when the modifier is moved around in the following series of sentences.

Only life exists on earth. *(There is nothing else on earth except life.)*

Life only exists on earth. *(Life does nothing but exist on earth.)*

Life exists only on earth. *(Nowhere else but on earth can one find life.)*

Life exists on earth only. *(More emphatic than the last sentence but says the same thing.)*

Place *only* and other modifiers close to the word that they modify. This is the best way to avoid ambiguity.

Split Infinitives

A split infinitive occurs when a modifier is placed between the sign of the infinitive "to" and the verb (*to better serve you*). In the italicized example, the infinitive "to serve" is split by the adverb "better." Careful writers try to avoid splitting infinitives.

Try to *not* split an infinitive.

The patient hopes to *fully* recover from pneumonia.

We want to *better* serve you.

Squinting Modifiers

A squinting modifier is one which is ambiguous because it is not clear whether it refers to the noun preceding it or the one following it.

NO: Women who like him sometimes gave him gifts.
YES: Women who like him gave him gifts sometimes.

NO: The professor sees juniors only on Fridays.
YES: The professor sees only juniors on Fridays.

Lack of Parallel Structure

When ideas are similar, they should be expressed in similar forms. When elements of a sentence are similar, they too should appear in similar form.

NO: She likes sun, the sand, and the sea.
YES: She likes the sun, the sand, and the sea.

NO: George is always singing, drumming, or he will play the guitar.
YES: George is always singing, drumming, or playing the guitar.

NO: Charlene's car skidded, turned sideways, then comes to a stop.
YES: Charlene's car skidded, turned sideways, and came to a stop.

Whenever *and* or *or* is used in a sentence, each must connect equal parts. Words are paired with words, phrases with phrases, clauses with clauses, and sentences with sentences. All these pairs must be *parallel;* they must have the same form.

> NO: Her family went to London, to Amsterdam, and they even saw Rome and Paris!
>
> YES: Her family went to London, to Amsterdam, and even to Rome and Paris!
>
> NO: You can use this form to apply or if you want to change your status.
>
> YES: You can use this form to apply or to change your status.
>
> NO: Debby noticed the way Margie talked and how she kept looking at the desk.
>
> YES: Debby noticed how Margie talked and how she kept looking at the desk.

Pairs of connectives, such as *both/and, either/or, neither/nor,* and *not only/ but also,* usually connect parallel structures.

> NO: That book was both helpful and contained a lot of information.
>
> YES: That book was both helpful and informative.
>
> NO: So, my father said, "Either you come with us now, or stay here alone."
>
> YES: So, my father said, "Either you come with us now, or you stay here alone."
>
> NO: Here we either turn left or right, but I forget which.
>
> YES: Here we turn either left or right, but I forget which.
>
> NO: Karen bought the table both for beauty and utility.
>
> YES: Karen bought the table for both beauty and utility.

Sentence Fragments

"Where did you go?"

"To the new movie theater. The one on Valley Street."

"Where on Valley Street?"

"Just past the train station, and across the street from the post office."

"See a good movie?"

"The best. Really funny, but serious, too."

"Sounds good."

Probably neither of the people in the conversation above realized that they were not using complete sentences. Only the first question, *"Where did you go?"* is a complete sentence. The rest are sentence fragments.

A sentence fragment is only a part of a sentence, because it is usually missing a subject or a verb.

NO:	So illogical!
YES:	It is so illogical!
NO:	Only for love, you see.
YES:	They did it only for love, you see.
NO:	No one. Not even the teacher.
YES:	No one, not even the teacher, could do it.

In conversation (as in the one above), there is a tendency to speak in sentence fragments, and so such fragments often appear in our writing. Proofreading and revision, however, can help to correct this error.

There are two ways to correct a sentence fragment. The first is to supply whatever is missing, as was done above. The other way is to attach the fragment to the sentence before or after it.

NO:	When I jog, especially in the early morning. I sometimes see the morning star.
YES:	When I jog, especially in the early morning, I sometimes see the morning star.
NO:	Because he was wrong. That's why he was embarrassed.
YES:	He was embarrassed because he was wrong.

NO:	Always and everywhere. She thought of him always and every- where.
YES:	Always and everywhere, she thought of him.

It is not always incorrect to use sentence fragments. They are used to reproduce conversation and are also quite effective as questions and exclamations. Some examples are

How absurd!

Now for some examples.

After all this? Not on your life!

The more we studied, the less we knew.

Although properly used sentence fragments can add spark, it is generally best to avoid using them except when more liveliness is needed.

Run-On Sentences

A run-on sentence contains two complete sentences totally fused.

NO:	It was a pleasant drive the sun was shining.
YES:	It was a pleasant drive because the sun was shining.
NO:	They are all similar materials they may not look or feel alike.
YES:	They are all similar materials, although they may not look or feel alike.
NO:	Susan said we passed the restaurant I think it's farther ahead.
YES:	Susan said we passed the restaurant. I think it's farther ahead.

Comma Splices

The run-on sentence is a very common error. Sometimes a writer will try to correct it by inserting a comma between the clauses, but this creates another error, a comma splice. The following examples illustrate various ways to correct the comma splice.

NO:	Talk softly, someone is listening.
YES:	Talk softly; someone is listening.

OR

Talk softly, for someone is listening.

NO:	If you know, you must tell us, we will do it.
YES:	If you know, you must tell us. Then we will do it.
NO:	Take a hint from me, drive more slowly on this curve.
YES:	Take a hint from me: drive more slowly on this curve.
NO:	We were lost, the captain could not see the land.
YES:	We were lost. The captain could not see the land.

Short, Choppy Sentences—Sentence Variation

Try to read the following passage:

> *There was a table set out under a tree. It was in front of the house. The March Hare and the Hatter were having tea at it. A Dormouse was sitting between them. He was fast asleep. The other two were using it as a cushion. They rested their elbows on it. They talked over its head. "Very uncomfortable for the Dormouse," thought Alice; "only, as it's asleep, I suppose it doesn't mind."*

Notice how quickly you read when the sentences are short; you hardly have enough time to form a picture of the scene. It is as if the writer added each thought as it occurred to him, and in fact, this is usually the case. It is a sure sign of poor writing. Now read the same excerpt the way that Lewis Carroll wrote it.

> *There was a table set out under a tree in front of the house, and the March Hare and the Hatter were having tea at it: a Dormouse was sitting between them, fast asleep, and the other two were using it as a cushion, resting their elbows on it and talking over its head. "Very*

*uncomfortable for the Dormouse," thought Alice; "only,
as it's asleep, I suppose it doesn't mind."*

Sentence variation creates well-balanced, smooth writing that flows and gives the reader the feeling that the writer knows the subject. Although there is nothing grammatically wrong with short sentences, they often separate ideas that should be brought together.

NO: People change. Places change. Alan felt this. He had been away for ten years.

YES: On returning after a ten-year absence, Alan had a strong feeling of how people and places change.

NO: She looked at the sky. Then she looked at the sea. They were too big. She threw a rock in the ocean. She started to cry. Then she went home.

YES: The sky and the sea looked too big. She threw a rock into the ocean, and as it disappeared she began to cry. Then she turned to go home.

As a rule, avoid using chains of short, choppy sentences. Organize your thoughts and try to vary the length of your sentences.

Wordiness

Effective writing means concise writing. Wordiness, on the other hand, decreases clarity of expression by cluttering sentences with unnecessary words. Of course, short sentences are not necessarily better than long ones simply because they are brief. As long as a word serves a function, it should remain in the sentence. However, repetition of words, sounds, and phrases should be used only for emphasis or other stylistic reasons. Editing your writing will reduce its bulk. Notice the difference in impact between the first and second sentences in the following pairs.

NO: The medical exam that he gave me was entirely complete.
YES: The medical exam he gave me was complete.

NO: It seems perfectly clear to me that although he went and got permission from the professor, he still should not have played that awful, terrible joke on the dean.
YES: It seems clear to me that although he got permission from the professor, he still should not have played that terrible joke on the dean.

NO: It will be our aim to ensure proper health care for each and every one of the people in the United States.
YES: Our aim will be to ensure proper health care for all Americans.

Rambling Sentences

A rambling sentence continues on and on and seems to never end.

NO: The mountain was steep, but the road was clear; the sun was shining, and we all had the spirit of adventure in our heart and a song of the open road on our lips, so we took the turn that took our car up that steep mountain road.
YES: The mountain was steep, but the road was clear. The sun was shining. All of us had the spirit of adventure in our heart and a song of the open road on our lips. So we took our car up that steep mountain road.

There is often nothing grammatically wrong with a rambling sentence; it is simply too long, and it interferes with the reader's comprehension. Unfortunately, a writer who makes this kind of error tends to do it a lot. A good rule to follow is this: If a sentence runs for more than two typewritten lines, think twice about it. It should probably be recast.

II. WORDS COMMONLY CONFUSED AND MISUSED

The complex nature of language sometimes makes writing difficult. Words often become confusing when they have similar forms and sounds. Indeed, an author may have a correct meaning in mind, but an incorrect word choice can alter the meaning of a sentence or even make it totally illogical.

> NO:	Martha was always part of that *cliché*.
> YES:	Martha was always part of that *clique*.
> (A *cliché* is a trite or hackneyed expression; a *clique* is an exclusive group of people.)

> NO:	The minister spoke of the soul's *immorality*.
> YES:	The minister spoke of the soul's *immortality*.
> (*Immorality* means wickedness; *immortality* means imperishable or unending life.)

> NO:	Where is the nearest *stationary* store?
> YES:	Where is the nearest *stationery* store?
> (*Stationary* means immovable; *stationery* is paper used for writing.)

Below are groups of words that are often confused because of their similar forms and sounds.

1. *a* — *A* is used before words beginning with a consonant sound.

   an — *An* is used before words with a vowel sound. This is an important distinction; it is not the spelling that determines whether to use *a* or *an*, but the sound.

   an umbrella BUT a university

   a radio BUT an RCA record

   an hour BUT a human being

   a historical event BUT an honorary degree

2. accent — v. to stress or emphasize. (You must *accent* the last syllable.)

	ascent	n. a climb or rise. (John's *ascent* of the mountain was dangerous.)
	assent	n. consent, compliance. (We need your *assent* before we can go ahead with the plans.)
3.	accept	v. to take something offered. (She *accepted* the gift.)
	except	prep. other than, but. (Everyone was included in the plans *except* him.)
4.	advice	n. opinion given as to what to do or how to handle a situation. (Her sister gave her *advice* on what to say at the interview.)
	advise	v. to counsel. (John's guidance counselor *advised* him on which colleges to apply to.)
5.	affect	v. to influence. (Mary's suggestion did not *affect* me.)
	effect	v. to cause to happen. (The plan was *effected* with great success.) n. result. (The *effect* of the medicine is excellent.)
6.	allusion	n. indirect reference. (In the poem, there are many biblical *allusions*.)
	illusion	n. false idea or conception; belief or opinion not in accord with the facts. (Greg was under the *illusion* that he could win the race after missing three weeks of practice.)

7. already   adv. previously. (I had *already* read that novel.)

    all ready   adv. + adj. prepared. (The family was *all ready* to leave on vacation.)

8. altar   n. table or stand used in religious rites. (The priest stood at the *altar.*)

    alter   v. to change. (Their plans were *altered* during the strike.)

9. as if   conj. as it would be if (It looks *as if* it's going to rain.)

    like   prep. inclined to (It looks *like* rain.)

10. capital   n. 1. a city where the government meets. (The senators had a meeting in Albany, the *capital* of New York.) 2. money used in business. (They had enough *capital* to develop the industry.)

    capitol   n. building in which the legislature meets. (Senator Brown gave a speech at the *Capitol* in Washington.)

11. choose   v. to select. (Which camera did you *choose*?)

    chose   past tense, choose. (Susan *chose* to stay home.)

12. cite   v. to quote. (The student *cited* evidence from the text.)

    site   n. location. (They chose the *site* where the house would be built.)

13. clothes   n. garments. (Because she got caught in the rain, her *clothes* were wet.)

cloths   n. pieces of material. (The *cloths* were used to wash the windows.)

14. coarse   adj. rough, unrefined. (Sandpaper is *coarse*.)

course   n. 1. path of action. (She did not know what *course* would solve the problem.)

2. passage. (We took the long *course* to the lake.)

3. series of studies. (We both enrolled in the physics *course*.)

4. part of a meal. (She served a five-*course* meal.)

15. consul   n. a person appointed by the government to live in a foreign city and represent the citizenry and business interests of the native country there. (The *consul* was appointed to Naples, Italy.)

council   n. a group used for discussion or advisement. (The *council* decided to accept his letter of resignation.)

counsel   v. to advise. (Tom *counsels* Jerry on tax matters.)

16. criterion   n. (singular) standard (The only *criterion* is patience.)

criteria   (plural) (There are several *criteria* applicants must meet.)

17. decent   adj. proper; respectable. (He was very *decent* about the entire matter.)

descent   n. 1. moving down. (In Dante's *Inferno*, the *descent* into hell was depicted graphically.) 2. ancestry. (He is of Irish *descent*.)

18. device   n. 1. plan; scheme. (The *device* helped her win the race.) 2. invention. (We bought a *device* that opens the garage door automatically.)

devise   v. to contrive. (He *devised* a plan so John could not win.)

19. emigrate   v. to go away from a country. (Many Japanese *emigrated* from Japan in the late 1800s.)

immigrate   v. to come into a country. (Her relatives *immigrated* to the United States after World War I.)

20. eminent   n. prominent. (He is an *eminent* member of the community.)

imminent   adj. impending. (The decision is *imminent*.)

immanent   adj. existing within. (Maggie believed that religious spirit is *immanent* in human beings.)

21. fair   adj. 1. beautiful. (She was a *fair* maiden.)

2. just. (She tried to be *fair*.)

n. festival. (There were many games at the *fair*.)

fare   n. amount of money paid for transportation. (The city proposed that the subway *fare* be raised.)

22. farther   adv. distance. (We travelled farther than we expected.)

     further   adv. furthermore; in depth. (We will discuss this *further*.)

23. forth   adv. onward. (The soldiers moved *forth* in the blinding snow.)

     fourth   adj. 4th. (She was the *fourth* runner-up in the beauty contest.)

24. imply   v. to suggest something. (I *implied* that I didn't approve of their actions.)

     infer   v. to drawer a conclusion from a remark or action. (I *inferred* from your letter that you will not be attending the meeting next week.)

25. insure   v. to guarantee. (He *insured* his luggage before the flight.)

     ensure   v. to make certain. (*Ensure* your safety by driving carefully.)

26. its   possessive form of *it*. (Our town must improve *its* roads.)

     it's   contraction of *it is*. (*It's* time to leave the party.)

27. later   adj., adv. at a subsequent date. (We will take a vacation *later* this year.)

     latter   n. second of the two. (Susan can visit Monday or Tuesday. The *latter*, however, is preferable.)

28. lead   n. a metal. (The handgun was made of *lead*.) v. to show the way. (The camp counselor *leads* the way to the picnic grounds.)

	led	past tense of verb *lead*. (The dog *led* the way.)
29.	lend	v. to let out for temporary use. (We are in the business of *lending* you money.)
	loan	n. money lent at interest. (The bank gave the student a *loan* for her tuition.)
30.	loose	adj. free, unrestricted. (The dog was let *loose* by accident.)
	lose	v. to suffer the loss of. (He was afraid he would *lose* the race.)
31.	moral	adj. virtuous. (She is a *moral* woman with high ethical standards.) n. lesson taught by a story, incident, etc. (Most fables end with a *moral.*)
	morale	n. mental condition. (After the team lost the game, their *morale* was low.)
32.	of	prep. from. (She is *of* French descent.)
	off	adv. away, at a distance. (The television fell *off* the table.)
33.	passed	past tense of verb *pass*. having satisfied some requirement. (He *passed* the test.)
	past	adj. gone by or elapsed in time. (His *past* deeds got him in trouble.) n. a period of time gone by. (His *past* was shady.) prep. beyond. (She ran *past* the house.)

34. personal   adj. private. (Jack was unwilling to discuss his childhood; it was too *personal*.)

      personnel   n. staff. (The *personnel* at the department store was made up of young adults.)

35. principal   n. head of a school. (The *principal* addressed the graduating class.) adj. main, most important. (JR was the *principal* character in the TV drama "Dallas.") or (The country's *principal* export is coffee.)

      principle   n. the ultimate source, origin, or cause of something; a law, truth. (The *principles* of physics were reviewed in class today.)

36. prophecy   n. prediction of the future. (His *prophecy* that he would become a doctor came true.)

      prophesy   v. to declare or predict. (He *prophesied* that we would win the lottery.)

37. quiet   adj. still; calm. (At night, all is *quiet*.)

      quite   adv. really, truly. (She is *quite* a good singer.)

      quit   v. to free oneself. (Peter had little time to spare, so he *quit* the chorus.)

38. respectfully   adv. with respect, honor, esteem. (He declined the offer *respectfully*.)

respectively	adv. in the order mentioned. (Jack, Susan, and Jim, who are members of the club, were elected president, vice president, and secretary, *respectively*.)
39. stationary	adj. immovable. (The park bench is *stationary*.)
stationery	n. paper used for writing. (The invitations were printed on yellow *stationery*.)
40. straight	adj. not curved. (The road was *straight*.)
strait	adj. restricted, narrow, confined. (The patient was put into a *strait* jacket.) n. narrow waterway. (He sailed through the *Straits* of Magellan.)
41. than	conj. used most commonly in comparisons. (Maggie is older *than* I.)
then	adv. soon afterward. (We lived in Boston; *then* we moved to New York.)
42. their	possessive form of *they*. (That is *their* house on Tenafly Drive.)
they're	contraction of *they are*. *(They're* leaving for California next week.)
there	adv. at that place. (Who is standing *there* under the tree?)
43. to	prep. in the direction of; toward. (She made a turn *to* the right onto Norman Street.)

	too	adv. 1. more than enough. (She served *too* much for dinner.) 2. also. (He is going to Maine *too.*)
	two	n. 2; the sum of one plus one. (We have *two* pet rabbits.)
44.	weather	n. the general condition of the atmosphere. (The *weather* is expected to be clear on Sunday.)
	whether	conj. if it be a case or fact. (We don't know *whether* the trains are late.)
45.	who's	contraction of *who is* or *who has.* (*Who's* willing to volunteer for the night shift?)
	whose	possessive form of *who.* (*Whose* book is this?)
46.	your	possessive form of *you.* (Is this *your* seat?)
	you're	contraction of *you are.* (I know *you're* going to do well on the test.)

APPENDICES

(sample appendix)

Appendix A

When a Paper has Only One Source

If a term paper is written using only one source, a special way to make notes of sources is used. The first footnote in the text is the only true footnote. This footnote will give the author's name, the title of the book, the page of the reference, and all of the publication information. For all notes after this first footnote, all the writer needs to do is place the page reference in parenthesis in the text where the note is needed. Because of this system, no bibliography is needed.

For example, a term paper using only The Scarlet Letter by Nathaniel Hawthorne would need a solitary footnote, shown below. All notes in the text that follow would have a structure such as: The soldiers were originally from the Niagara frontier (p. 23) but Roger Chillingworth lived in Oxford (p. 121).

If the term paper used a play for its only source, such as Shakespeare's Hamlet, then the notes after the first footnote would contain act, scene, and line references (I, ii, 23-30) instead of a page reference. An example would be: Hamlet makes reference to another of Shakespeare's classics Julius Caesar (III, ii, 109-110).

---

1. Nathaniel Hawthorne, The Scarlet Letter (New York: Barnes & Noble, Inc., 1993) 21.

Appendix B

Words and phrases to use in transitions

Addition: in addition, also, added to, additionally, then, another, further-more, finally, next, and, besides, equally important, similarly, moreover

Contrast: but, yet, however, although, on the other hand, at the same time, in contrast, nevertheless, notwithstanding, conversely, nonethe-less

Example: for example, for instance, to illustrate, specifically, thus, in par-ticular, in other words, namely

Comparison: likewise, similarly, in like manner, in comparison, both, in the same way

Concession: of course, certainly, granted, naturally, while, although, to be sure, notwithstanding, in spite of

Time sequence: first, firstly, next, when, at the same time, second, secondly, soon, later, during, meanwhile, subsequently, at length, eventu-ally, currently, immediately

Summary: as a result, hence, in short, in brief, in other words, in conclusion, finally, since, on the whole, for these reasons

Result: therefore, accordingly, so, consequently, due to this, thus

Place: in the foreground, here, there, adjacent, nearby, in the distance, in the front, in the background

SAMPLE
BIBLIOGRAPHY

(sample bibliography)

Bibliography

Angelou, Maya. I Know Why the Caged Bird Sings. New York: Random House, 1969.

de la Croix, Horst et al. Art Through the Ages. Eighth edition, New York: Harcourt Brace Jovanovich, Publishers, vol. I, 1982.

Dible, Donald M., ed. What Everybody Should Know About Patents, Trademarks and Copyrights. Fairfield: The Entrepreneur Press, 1978.

Fitzgerald, Frances Scott. The Great Gatsby. New York: Charles Scribner's Sons, 1925.

Winchester, A.M. Modern Biology. Second edition, New York: Van Nostrand Reinhold Company, 1971.

Weinberg, Robert A. "Tumor Suppresser Genes." Science. American Association for the Advancement of Science, vol. 254, Nov. 22, 1991.

Checklist

1. *Timing:* The student should make sure his paper is on time. Most instructors give lower grades to late papers.

2. *Length:* Most research papers are too short. The student should make sure that the paper is long enough.

3. *Footnotes:* The student should make sure that footnotes are in the correct form and are properly placed.

4. *Bibliography:* The bibliography should also be in the correct form. The student should be sure that he has used enough sources. Some professors specify a minimum number of sources to use.

5. *Presentation:* The research paper should be neatly typed or word processed. Generally, margins should be one inch left and right and the paper should be double-spaced. Pages should be numbered and a title page should be included.

6. *Instructions:* The student should be certain that he has met all of the criteria set by his instructor. He should also meet the specifications of this book.

NOTES

NOTES

NOTES

NOTES

NOTES